*Greater Tha
available in Ebook and ....   t.

Greater Than a Tourist Book Series
Reviews from Readers

I think the series is wonderful and beneficial for tourists to get information before visiting the city.

-Seckin Zumbul, Izmir Turkey

I am a world traveler who has read many trip guides but this one really made a difference for me. I would call it a heartfelt creation of a local guide expert instead of just a guide.

-Susy, Isla Holbox, Mexico

New to the area like me, this is a must have!

-Joe, Bloomington, USA

This is a good series that gets down to it when looking for things to do at your destination without having to read a novel for just a few ideas.

-Rachel, Monterey, USA

Good information to have to plan my trip to this destination.

-Pennie Farrell, Mexico

Great ideas for a port day.

-Mary Martin USA

Aptly titled, you won't just be a tourist after reading this book. You'll be greater than a tourist!

-Alan Warner, Grand Rapids, USA

Even though I only have three days to spend in San Miguel in an upcoming visit, I will use the author's suggestions to guide some of my time there. An easy read - with chapters named to guide me in directions I want to go.

-Robert Catapano, USA

Great insights from a local perspective! Useful information and a very good value!

-Sarah, USA

This series provides an in-depth experience through the eyes of a local. Reading these series will help you to travel the city in with confidence and it'll make your journey a unique one.

-Andrew Teoh, Ipoh, Malaysia

>TOURIST

GREATER THAN A TOURIST- GUANACASTLE COSTA RICA

50 Travel Tips from a Local

Courtney Hall

Greater Than a Tourist-Guanacaste Costa Rica Copyright © 2020 by CZYK Publishing LLC. All Rights Reserved.

All rights reserved. No part of this book may be reproduced in any form or by any electronic or mechanical means including information storage and retrieval systems, without permission in writing from the author. The only exception is by a reviewer, who may quote short excerpts in a review.

The statements in this book are of the authors and may not be the views of CZYK Publishing or Greater Than a Tourist.

First Edition

Cover designed by: Ivana Stamenkovic

Cover Image: https://pixabay.com/photos/witches--rock-guanacaste-costa-rica-1060816/

Image 1: taken by author

Image 2: https://unsplash.com/photos/IEg0YUk_xfc Photo by Jonathan Segal on Unsplash

Image 3: https://unsplash.com/photos/Uk9sorBelfg Photo by Courtney Hall on Unsplash

Image 4: https://unsplash.com/photos/NFuNPHndDO8 Photo by Josué Barboza on Unsplash

Image 5: https://unsplash.com/photos/Dmvnnt-nfkA Photo by Yannick Menard on Unsplash

CZYK Publishing Since 2011.
Greater Than a Tourist

Lock Haven, PA
All rights reserved.

ISBN: 9798633385281

>TOURIST

50 TRAVEL TIPS FROM A LOCAL

>TOURIST

BOOK DESCRIPTION

With travel tips and culture in our guidebooks written by a local, it is never too late to visit Guanacaste. Most travel books tell you how to travel like a tourist. Although there is nothing wrong with that, as part of the 'Greater Than a Tourist' series, this book will give you candid travel tips from someone who has lived at your next travel destination. This guide book will not tell you exact addresses or store hours but instead gives you knowledge that you may not find in other smaller print travel books. Experience cultural, culinary delights, and attractions with the guidance of a Local. Slow down and get to know the people with this invaluable guide. By the time you finish this book, you will be eager and prepared to discover new activities at your next travel destination.

Inside this travel guide book you will find:

Visitor information from a Local
Tour ideas and inspiration
Save time with valuable guidebook information

Greater Than a Tourist- A Travel Guidebook with 50 Travel Tips from a Local. Slow down, stay in one place, and get to know the people and culture. By the time you finish this book, you will be eager and prepared to travel to your next destination.

OUR STORY

Traveling is a passion of the Greater than a Tourist book series creator. Lisa studied abroad in college, and for their honeymoon Lisa and her husband toured Europe. During her travels to Malta, an older man tried to give her some advice based on his own experience living on the island since he was a young boy. She was not sure if she should talk to the stranger but was interested in his advice. When traveling to some places she was wary to talk to locals because she was afraid that they weren't being genuine. Through her travels, Lisa learned how much locals had to share with tourists. Lisa created the Greater Than a Tourist book series to help connect people with locals. A topic that locals are very passionate about sharing.

TABLE OF CONTENTS

BOOK DESCRIPTION
OUR STORY
TABLE OF CONTENTS
DEDICATION
ABOUT THE AUTHOR
HOW TO USE THIS BOOK
FROM THE PUBLISHER
WELCOME TO > TOURIST
1. Best time to visit Guanacaste
2. How to get around
3. Airports
4. Currency
5. Tipping
6. Budget
7. Staying connected
8. Climate/Weather in Guanacaste
9. Tico/Tica
10. Pura Vida
11. Costa Rican Spanish is more formal in Guanacaste
12. Other Slang vocabulary to know:
13. The Guanacaste tree is the national tree
14. The economy is pretty good, but unemployment is high, especially in Guanacaste

15. The country is incredibly biodiverse & a leader in environmental protections
16. They have no army!
17. Holidays & cultural events in Costa Rica
18. Sunscreen & bug spray
19. Beach towns are casual
20. Public Transportation, Ubers, and Taxis:
21. Addresses are overrated
22. Late night beach walks - not the best idea
23. Protect your valuables or leave them at home
24. Your rental car
25. Driving tips
26. Check out the local food and eat at a Soda:
27. A hearty Costa Rican breakfast
28. What to do if you're Gluten intolerant
29. Tips for Vegetarians/Vegans
30. Need to see a doctor?
31. See an animal in need?
32. Where to surf
33. What to bring with you (and leave at the hotel)
34. Watch the sunset
35. Playa Conchal
36. Playa Brasilito
37. Playa Tamarindo
38. Playa Samara
39. Playa Nosara

>TOURIST

40. Sea turtle "arribada" at Ostional Wildlife Refuge
41. Monteverde Cloud Forest
42. Diria Coffee Farm Tour
43. Llanos de Cortez Waterfall
44. Las Catalinas
45. Rincon de la Vieja
46. Arenal Volcano & town of La Fortuna
47. Adventure Travel
48. Volunteering in Costa Rica
49. Namaste or *Naw, Imma Stay* (in Costa Rica)?
50. LGBTQ+ Travel

TOP REASONS TO BOOK THIS TRIP

Packing and Planning Tips

Travel Questions

Travel Bucket List

NOTES

DEDICATION

This book is dedicated to Mike for his openness to new adventures and continued support that make living on Costa Rica so wonderful.

To the volunteers and staff at Abriendo Mentes, and the residents of Brasilito and Potrero, thank you for embracing us.

To my parents and family members who have supported us in our decision to move to Costa Rica: you can visit anytime!

ABOUT THE AUTHOR

Courtney Hall is a Colorado native who lives in Guanacaste, Costa Rica with her partner, Mike, beloved dog and two feline friends. An avid traveler and global health professional, Courtney has worked in non-profits and health research for most of her career.

Courtney decided she couldn't put off her dreams of living internationally any longer and quit her 9-5 job and relocated to Costa Rica. In 2019, she launched her Etsy store, Sense of Wonder Designs, where she hopes to nurture and inspire a love for travel through photography and graphic design.

She also works as a consultant for start-ups and entrepreneurs in the health industry.

You can see more of her work at lifestoocourt.com.

>TOURIST

HOW TO USE THIS BOOK

The *Greater Than a Tourist* book series was written by someone who has lived in an area for over three months. The goal of this book is to help travelers either dream or experience different locations by providing opinions from a local. The author has made suggestions based on their own experiences. Please check before traveling to the area in case the suggested places are unavailable.

Travel Advisories: As a first step in planning any trip abroad, check the Travel Advisories for your intended destination.
https://travel.state.gov/content/travel/en/traveladvisories/traveladvisories.html

FROM THE PUBLISHER

Traveling can be one of the most important parts of a person's life. The anticipation and memories that you have are some of the best. As a publisher of the Greater Than a Tourist, as well as the popular *50 Things to Know* book series, we strive to help you learn about new places, spark your imagination, and inspire you. Wherever you are and whatever you do I wish you safe, fun, and inspiring travel.

Lisa Rusczyk Ed. D.
CZYK Publishing

>TOURIST

WELCOME TO
> TOURIST

>TOURIST

Taken by author

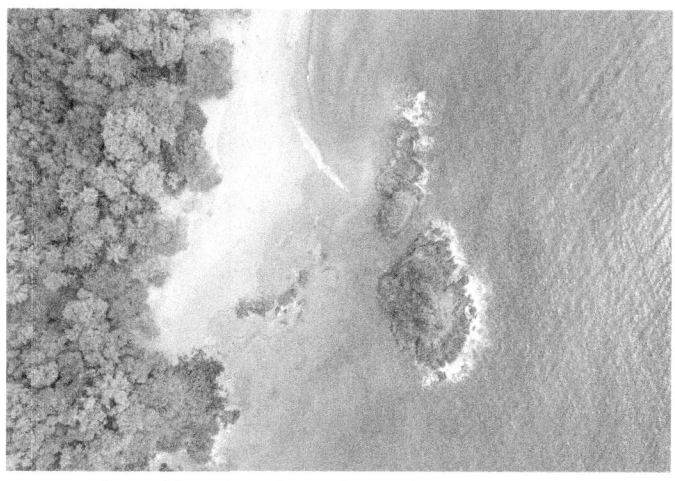
Drone flight above Manuel Antonio, Costa Rica

Palm trees in Manuel Antonio, Costa Rica

>TOURIST

Manuel Antonio C.R

Beaches of Costa Rica

>TOURIST

"Travel isn't always pretty. It isn't always comfortable. Sometimes it hurts, it even breaks your heart. But that's okay. The journey changes you; it should change you. It leaves marks on your memory, on your consciousness, on your heart, and on your body. You take something with you. Hopefully, you leave something good behind."

- Anthony Bourdain

The secret's out! Costa Rica is one of the top travel destinations searched online and it's easy to see why. Here, you can seek adventure, relaxation and rejuvenation in Guanacaste, Costa Rica by experiencing unspoiled nature, a friendly and welcoming culture, and a slower pace of living. In this book, I share my top tips to experience Guanacaste's friendly people, pristine shoreline, unparalleled wildlife and diverse geography. There is something for everyone in this beautiful Central American country.

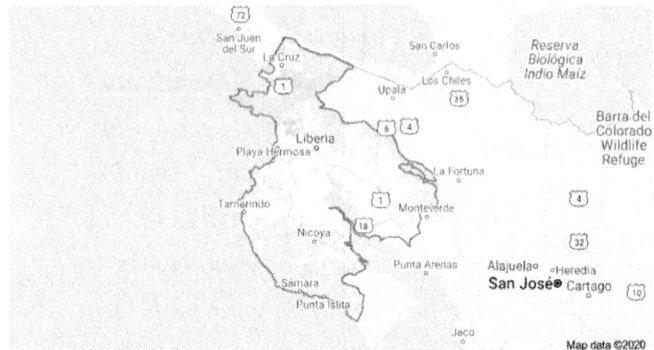

Guanacaste Province
Costa Rica

\>TOURIST

Guanacaste Province Climate

	High	Low
January	91	71
February	92	72
March	94	73
April	95	75
May	92	74
June	89	74
July	89	73
August	89	73
September	87	72
October	87	72
November	88	71
December	89	70

GreaterThanaTourist.com

Temperatures are in Fahrenheit degrees.
Source: NOAA

>TOURIST

THE BASICS:

1. BEST TIME TO VISIT GUANACASTE

There's really never a bad time to come to Costa Rica, but here's what you need to know to plan the best time for you. As the driest province in the country, Guanacaste receives almost no rain for 10 months out of the year. This means constant sunshine and hot temperatures! The exception to this is September and October, which is the height of the rainy season. During the rainy season, everything is lush and green just like the rest of the country. The days may be a little bit more overcast and bursts of rain will occur on most days. I love this time of year because it's when you get a break from the heat and the frogs come out to sing.

The "high tourist season" stretches from December - April, when most international tourists come to flee the colder climates of the northern latitudes. Having lived here a full year, July is the best time to plan a beach vacation in Guanacaste, in my opinion. By July, some rain will have finally arrived in the region, breathing new life into the flora and fauna. The rains are also infrequent and short enough that you can go to the beach before or after and still experience full days of sunshine. Another perk of traveling in the off season is that getting around & finding accommodation is easier and prices for excursions and activities will be a little more affordable.

2. HOW TO GET AROUND

I definitely suggest renting a car, and if you do, it should be an SUV. While Costa Rica's roads have improved a lot in recent years, there are still potholes and some hairier stretches of unpaved or damaged roads that can cause some serious damage to your car. There are also roads with steep grades so an SUV that has the strength to get you up that hill is *muy importante*. Almost all roads between major destinations are paved and you will be thankful for the air conditioning in between activities.

As the most sparsely populated region of Costa Rica, I would advise against public transportation, especially if you don't want to lose valuable vacation time traveling from point A to point B. Busses often run only once per hour or less, and it's rare that they

>TOURIST

arrive on time so you can experience long wait times in the heat. It's also important to note that while there may be some taxis in the Guanacaste region, there are little to no Ubers (unless you're in a larger city like Liberia).

To rent a car, you can get one when you arrive at the airport - but it's best to reserve them ahead of time, as there tends to be shortages of rental cars in the high season. You can also opt to get one once you're at your destination, as there are rental companies in the major beach towns. Keep in mind Costa Rica requires two types of insurance (3rd Party Liability and a Collision Damage Waiver) which may not be included in the daily rates you receive in your quote online. Because of this, many people that come to Costa Rica expecting to get a good deal on a rental are in for a big surprise when it comes time to hand over that credit card. To avoid any big surprises, call the rental companies and ask them about it. You can also get part of the insurance fee waived if you book the car with a credit card that offers coverage as a benefit. You will have to provide proof of this, but this can save you $10-15/day on a car rental. Further, plan for rentals to cost more than what's quoted when you're comparing prices and be prepared to leave a refundable deposit when you pick up the car on your credit card. I recommend asking your rental company questions about these things before coming to Costa Rica, so you're prepared with all the necessary paperwork.

3. AIRPORTS

LIR vs SJO – To get to Guanacaste, Liberia's Daniel Oduber International Airport is the one to choose. Although it is the smaller of the two and usually has fewer, and more expensive flights, the location of LIR is much more convenient. You can be at the beaches of the Pacific Coast in only 45 minutes and many resorts and hotels offer shuttle services that will pick up and drop off at the airport. If you choose to fly into San Jose, you can drive into Guanacaste in about 4 hours. I recommend giving yourself enough time to stop at places like Monteverde, Arenal, or Rincon de la Vieja for a day or two before heading to the beach towns (keep reading for more info on these towns!).

>TOURIST
4. CURRENCY

USD vs Colones - The local currency of Costa Rica is the Colon. Although this is the national currency, most places also accept US dollars. This means, don't waste your time and money exchanging at a bank ahead of time or at the exchange kiosks at the airport. In fact, you can withdraw USD and Colones at most ATMs here. The catch is that if you do spend US dollars, you will likely receive your change back in Colones and the exchange rate is up to the business' discretion. On the flip side, you can also *save* some money paying for activities in cash over a credit card. If you decide to use credit or withdraw cash when you get here, be sure to check that your card has no foreign transaction fees or ATM withdrawal fees. This way you will get the best exchange rate, avoid unnecessary fees and not have to carry around large sums of cash. *(CapitalOne 360 FTW!)* A mobile app that I recommend is a currency app that will convert prices to your local currency, and most importantly, colones to USD. This way you can see just how much that jar of peanut butter is when it says ₡3,670.

5. TIPPING

If you're visiting from a country where it's not customary to tip, it may come as a surprise, but you will find that many restaurants, tour guides, and hotel staff hope to receive a tip. You can tip in Colones, USD or when you pay with a credit card. On a receipt, you will see a line that says "propina" ('tip' in Spanish) where you can opt to leave a tip. But before tipping 15-20%, take a look at your receipt for a 10% service charge. This is a gratuity automatically added to your bill. I suggest adding an additional 5-10%, especially if your service was exceptional.

There was a story in 2019 that made headlines when a dentist from Winnipeg, who was traveling in Tamarindo, Costa Rica with his family, was accidentally charged $4000 for two servings of ice cream![1] What he didn't catch at the time, is that the employee accidentally charged the amount in USD instead of colones. The good news is he did end up getting reimbursed by his bank in the end. So, while it

---

[1] https://www.iheartradio.ca/580-cfra/news/dentist-overcharged-more-than-5k-for-ice-cream-gets-reimbursed-by-bank-1.10476352

isn't likely that something like this will happen to you, the lesson here is that accidents *can and do* happen, especially when dealing with conversion rates between two currencies. Lesson learned: always take a peek at your receipt and double check that your receipt reflects your purchases and the currency correctly so there aren't any surprises.

6. BUDGET

Contrary to what some may think, Costa Rica is 'muy caro' (very expensive) - Depending on where you're coming from and your travel preferences, it can be a little more difficult to save your money for those souvenirs. After living in cities with a high cost of living like Denver, CO, Sydney, Australia, and Washington DC, things like rent (long term) are definitely lower, especially when you consider proximity to the beach. In general, I don't find that I save any money by living here because where you may save *some* money on *some* expenses, others like buying a car, costs double!

For backpackers and budget travelers, there are hostels, cabinas, and homestays that are sure to fit into your budget. Homestays are also great because you will have the opportunity to practice your Spanish and immerse yourself in Costa Rican culture. Homestays often include your meals too, so you can enjoy some traditional, home cooking as well. YUMMMM!

Travelers who have a limited daily budget on food can also save money by eating like a local. Meaning, buy produce from local fruit & veg stands and enjoy Costa Rican cuisine at Costa Rican owned restaurants (called Sodas). There, you'll find large, hearty entrées called Casados for much less than what you'd pay for a meal at a chain restaurant or places in touristy beach towns. There are also opportunities to try some street food, which is a budget friendly option, but I haven't personally tried them as I'm a vegetarian. (Continue on for vegan/vegetarian tips below!)

For those who are looking for all-inclusive vacations, luxury resorts and vacation rentals, there are fantastic accommodations all along the coast, including vacation rentals with ocean views and infinity pools. Talk about amazing sunsets! I highly recommend these vacation rentals for families & groups as opposed to staying at hotels because it gives you more flexibility and privacy. Although there are some very nice hotels like Hacienda

>TOURIST

Guachipelin, the RIU Grand Palace, Diria Tamarindo, and boutique style accommodations.

Dining out, prices for a meal are on par with most US restaurants (in other words, you probably won't save money on most restaurants here). You can also hire private chefs who will cook for your group in your vacation rental or lead a cooking class, which is a popular choice for many tourists here.

Whether you're a budget traveler or luxury globetrotter, there's something for everyone.

7. STAYING CONNECTED

With cellular companies now offering international data for travelers, staying connected while you travel is easier than ever. However, keep in mind you will likely have slower data speeds than if you are using a local SIM card. If your cellular provider doesn't offer free data while you travel, I recommend unlocking your mobile device before coming to Costa Rica and buying a local SIM card. This will allow you to use GPS as well as call and text within the country. Speaking of GPS, Google Maps and WAZE are the best apps for navigation, despite the fact that there aren't any addresses in Costa Rica (but more on that later). The most widely used messaging app is WhatsApp so I'd download that from the app store before coming to Costa Rica as well.

As a T-Mobile customer, I have international data roaming at no extra cost with my plan. I opted to keep my T-Mobile plan instead of swapping out for a new SIM card when I came here. With my US phone number, I can make calls within Costa Rica for no extra charge and use unlimited data. The downside is its typically slower speeds. If I need to make a call to the US, I make sure I'm on Wi-Fi and rely on apps like Skype or Zoom to stay connected abroad.

8. CLIMATE/WEATHER IN GUANACASTE

There is one word to describe Guanacaste's climate: HOT! It is the driest & hottest part of Costa Rica and temperatures will be in the 90's F (30-35 C) all year round. If traveling to other parts of Costa Rica during your trip, keep in mind that Costa Rica has micro-climates. So, while it may be really hot and dry in most of Guanacaste, 2 hours inland it can be more humid, 5-10 F cooler, and more likely to rain. I recommend lightweight, cotton fabrics, quick dry materials, and of course your swimming gear like UPF shirts and coverups. Things like hats, fans, a water bottle and sunscreen will also come in handy in this region.

TALK LIKE A TICO:

9. TICO/TICA

Tico = Costa Rican man; *Tica* = Costa Rican woman

Tico is a colloquial term to describe a native person of Costa Rica, which you will hear more often than simply "Costa Rican" when describing the people. It's not used in a derogatory way and simply how Ticos refer to themselves. If you're a Spanish speaker, you may also hear Ticos adding 'tico' to the end of Spanish words that end with *-ito* or *-ita*. This is a fun little fact about Costa Rican Spanish slang that I like to share, especially for those interested in practicing their Spanish. For example, instead of saying "chiquito" when something is *really small*, they may say "chiquitico." This is a great way to impress the locals with your Costa Rican Spanish skills!

10. PURA VIDA

This is the national saying of Costa Rica that translates to "pure life". It is a term which represents the laid back, low stress mindset of the Costa Rican people. You can find this phrase written on a lot of souvenirs and t-shirts. You will also hear it used frequently in conversation as a greeting, farewell, and everything in between. A lesser known fact is that this phrase actually came from a 1956 Mexican film called *Pura Vida* and for some reason, Costa Ricans liked it so much, it stuck in the vernacular.

11. COSTA RICAN SPANISH IS MORE FORMAL IN GUANACASTE

When in doubt, use 'Usted.' Generally, in Costa Rica, Spanish is more formal. Here, usted is the default pronoun and is used in almost every situation. Even when addressing small children, adults will use this form. It is rare you will hear someone use the tu form when speaking with you unless they are a close friend. Usually though, the use of tu in a conversation is a dead giveaway that you are not Costa Rican. As a general rule, I always address others with the usted form and only respond with tu if someone uses the more informal vernacular with me first.

While we're on the subject, Costa Ricans substitute 'dar' with 'regalar' when ordering food or asking for directions. To order food in Costa Rica, you can use the verb *regalar* when ordering your Casado, a drink, and even asking for the bill. This is pretty funny when you think about it because it sounds as if you believe receiving a bill for your meal is a gift, rather than an obligation. Nonetheless, this is just another one of the endearing aspects of the Costa Rican vernacular. However, make a mental note that this is unique to Costa Rica. If you were to say '¿Me regala la cuenta por favor?' in another Spanish speaking country it will likely result in some funny looks.

12. OTHER SLANG VOCABULARY TO KNOW:

Tuanis = cool, nice, fine, okay

Mae = bro, dude

Que chiva! = How cool! (Chiva is pronounced like 'cheeba')

Goma = hangover

Guaro = booze, also a Costa Rican liquor made from sugar cane

Que madre! = Bummer!

Que salidas! = How crazy!, What nonsense!

Facts about Guanacaste and Costa Rica:

13. THE GUANACASTE TREE IS THE NATIONAL TREE

The namesake of this province, it was dubbed the national tree in 1959. It's also called the Elephant Ear tree because they are very large trees with a spherical crown. I think it looks more like an umbrella or a mushroom. Because of its large trunk size, you'll also see many tables made out of natural edged slabs of the wood. Many talented woodworkers make beautiful solid wood furniture, popular in Costa Rican homes. Fortunately, they produce quality, durable materials that last a long time in this climate.

14. THE ECONOMY IS PRETTY GOOD, BUT UNEMPLOYMENT IS HIGH, ESPECIALLY IN GUANACASTE

Costa Rica has had a stable economy for quite some time, despite its high unemployment rate (about 11%).[2] Agricultural exports like bananas, coffee, and

---

[2] https://ticotimes.net/2019/10/31/unemployment-in-costa-rica-registers-slight-decline-but-remains-high-at-11-4

sugar have historically been Costa Rica's backbone, however, tourism has rapidly grown into a prominent industry. Unfortunately, poverty is also high at about 21%[3] but it is also the lowest poverty rate in Central America.

15. THE COUNTRY IS INCREDIBLY BIODIVERSE & A LEADER IN ENVIRONMENTAL PROTECTIONS

Costa Rica is one of the most biodiverse countries, despite its small geographic size (it's little bit smaller than the US state of West Virginia and a little bit bigger than the country of Denmark, for comparison's sake). Here, 25% of the country is set aside as protected land, including national parks, reserves, and wildlife refuges. Because of this, Costa Rica is recognized worldwide for being at the forefront of conservation to protect its lush biodiversity.

In 2019, Costa Rica's President Carlos Alvarado Quesada announced plans to rid the country of fossil

---

[3] https://ticotimes.net/2019/10/18/poverty-remains-stable-at-21-in-costa-rica-government-says

fuels by 2050. If successful, Costa Rica could be the world's first 'zero emissions' country. Further, they continue to set records for recycling[4] and operate almost exclusively on renewable energy.[5] That same year, Costa Rica banned the import and sales of polystyrene packaging (Styrofoam), a law that will go into effect in 2021.[6]

In contrast to the country's reputation of being environmentally friendly and promoting sustainable practices, trash and littering remain a problem. Evidence of the lack of a sustainable solid waste management system can be seen throughout the country, in local communities and rivers. In Guanacaste specifically, several municipalities do not provide garbage collection yet. It is not uncommon to

---

[4] https://ticotimes.net/2019/01/29/its-official-costa-rica-sets-world-record-for-recycling

[5] https://ticotimes.net/2019/09/24/costa-rica-will-run-on-more-than-98-renewable-energy-for-fifth-consecutive-year-government-says

[6] https://www.newscientist.com/article/2210341-costa-rica-is-banning-the-use-of-polystyrene-packaging-from-2021/

see piles of trash and leaves burning on the side of the road or old appliances dumped. Furthermore, the Tarcoles River is the most contaminated river in Central America, due to dumping that takes place in San Jose and carries the trash 69 miles (111 km) to the beaches of Puntarenas.

While Costa Rica has made significant strides and continues to be a leader in sustainability, there are still areas for improvement. To do your part when traveling here, get involved in a local beach cleanup or plan one of your own, avoid single use plastics, and travel with your own reusable, stainless steel straws. Also limit use of electricity by turning your a/c off when you're not in your Airbnb or hotel room.

16. THEY HAVE NO ARMY!

There was a revolution in 1948 that lasted only 40 days but was Costa Rica's bloodiest conflict since it's declaration as an independent nation. After the National Liberation Army's victory, the new president, José Figueres Ferrer, abolished the army that same year. It was later encoded in Costa Rica's constitution in 1949. As a symbolic gesture for Costa

>TOURIST

Rica's future, President José Figueres Ferrer held a ceremony dedicating the former military barracks to a national museum. At the end of the ceremony, he handed the keys to the minister of education and announced the military budget would be redirected toward healthcare, education, and environmental protection.

Now, when dignitaries from other countries arrive, they are welcomed to the country by school children wearing the visitor's national colors. The country is often referred to as the "Switzerland of Central America" because it also serves as a neutral party in disputes among countries in this region.

17. HOLIDAYS & CULTURAL EVENTS IN COSTA RICA

Some important holidays and cultural events to note are the annual Fiestas, Semana Santa ("Holy Week") in April, and Guanacaste Day. Every year there are local rodeos held from December – March called Fiestas. These are annual bull riding festivals which take place in the town plaza all across Guanacaste including Brasilito, Potrero, Huacas, Villareal, Matapalo, and more. In April, Semana

Santa is a weeklong holiday leading up to the Easter holiday. For Ticos, it is a popular holiday for families to travel to the beaches for the week, particularly Playa Brasilito. It's best to not plan a vacation during this week to avoid the crowds. Lastly, Guanacaste Day (The Annexation of Guanacaste) is celebrated on July 25th. There are celebrations all across the province of Guanacaste to commemorate the annexation of Guanacaste to Costa Rica in 1824. This annexation occurred by choice by Guanacastecos and is now a nationwide public holiday. It is customary for schools and colleges to hold a ceremony, sell typical foods, crafts and have celebratory parades.

WHAT TO PACK:

18. SUNSCREEN & BUG SPRAY

I recommend buying this at home and bringing with you, as these items are pretty costly in Costa Rica. In Guanacaste, it's hot, hot, hot so you'll be sweating off that sunscreen. Don't forget to reapply! The same goes for bug spray although in the dry season mosquitoes are less prevalent so come prepared depending on which season you're traveling in. Of course, you can always buy more if you need it once you're here.

19. Beach towns are casual

While most people spend their days outside and at the beach, your swim attire, cover ups, and lightweight clothing will be your go-to's on your Costa Rica vacay. Since it is hot, you might go through clothing more quickly so it's never a bad idea to bring some detergent or dryer sheets to keep your clothes fresh. For a night on the town, you may want one outfit to get gussied up, but chances are, you're going to end up at the beach which means you'll be walking in the sand. Around here, putting on our nicest sandals is our version of getting dressed up. Locals and tourists alike get by with shorts and flip flops year-round so no need to dress to impress.

GETTING AROUND:

20. PUBLIC TRANSPORTATION, UBERS, AND TAXIS:

There is a bus system here, which offers affordable transportation across the country. In general, it may not be the most comfortable ride because of the heat, nor will it be the most time efficient. Navigating the bus system can also be confusing if you don't speak Spanish. You can take several buses to get to the beach towns, but as it requires switching bus lines, this adds to your travel time.

Apps like Uber work in Costa Rica but have not yet made their way to the beach towns of Guanacaste. You may find a car or two, but it won't be a reliable way to get around here just yet. They are more prevalent in the Central Valley and capital city of San Jose. Some of the larger and more touristy towns will have a handful of Ubers available, (so now, Tamarindo has a few) but most beach towns are also very walkable so I wouldn't expect to spend much time needing a car if you're staying within the town.

Another option is taking a '*colectivo*' which is *almost* like taking an Uber pool, but without the app. However, they are typically small, old and run-down cars. If you're standing on the side of the road and see a someone driving toward you, slowing down, and flashing his headlights at you, don't be nervous. They are just signaling that they are available to give you a ride if you need one. I traveled exclusively by *colectivo* and bus between Tamarindo and Potrero for 5 months and it helped me improve my Spanish and to learn my way around town.

Some useful guidelines when taking a *colectivo*: always ask for prices *before* you get into the car and know that you can negotiate. It is not uncommon for *colectivo* drivers to charge more if they can tell you're a tourist. You will also stop to pick up other riders on the way.

21. ADDRESSES ARE OVERRATED

If you ask for (or need to give) directions, it's important to know there are no addresses in Costa Rica. Giving good directions relies on landmarks so you may hear descriptions of a place that sound something like: "The green house on the right side, 250 meters west of the plaza." Fortunately, you can usually find the location of your destination within Waze or Google Maps just by searching the name of the business or vacation rental. Make sure you have either of those downloaded and cellular data on your phone and you'll be good to go! If you won't have data and you're worried about navigation, many rental car companies will offer a GPS device for an additional fee.

SAFETY TIPS

22. LATE NIGHT BEACH WALKS – NOT THE BEST IDEA

Depending on where you are, I don't recommend walking the beach at night. You never know what can happen, but just use your best judgment. Generally speaking, though, public beaches are not safe places at night, particularly for a solo female.

>TOURIST

23. PROTECT YOUR VALUABLES OR LEAVE THEM AT HOME

While it's always best to leave valuables at home, if you must bring something valuable like a camera, GoPro, or your phone even, do your best to hide your valuables safe from looky-loos. This includes in your rental car and on the beach. Petty theft is very common, and the best defense is to not make it obvious you have valuables or easy for anyone to run off with them.

24. YOUR RENTAL CAR

Get in the habit of making sure you don't leave any valuables visible and bring them with you when you can. In some places, there may be security where you park your car, but for the most part, there is not. In many places, people will approach you when you get out of your car and ask you for money to "watch" your car. It's usually best to just pay them 1-2,000 colones, even if it's unclear whether it's a legitimate operation. I also recommend you read the fine print of your rental agreement to know the ins and outs of what you may be responsible for in case something happens to the car.

25. DRIVING TIPS

Almost all roads are a single lane in either direction. In the beach towns, it is rare you will see a stop light so there are some speed demons out there. To control traffic, there are usually some strategically placed speed bumps but other than that people will often go over the speed limit. People tend to pass slower traffic, so just be aware that someone may try to drive around you. Typical driving rules apply here, just like everywhere else – don't pass someone when going around a corner, stop at the stop signs, yield when you need to yield, etc. Keep in mind, there aren't usually any streetlights and driving places at night it can get VERY dark. So, use those brights if you have to, to look out for people walking alongside the roads (there aren't any sidewalks here) and for wildlife.

COSTA RICAN FOOl

26. CHECK OUT THE LOCAL FOOD AND EAT AT A SODA:

When I first came to CR, I kept seeing roadside signs advertising "Sodas." *Wow, they really like carbonated beverages here*, I thought to myself. I soon found out that a "soda" is not a drink - it is a Costa Rican word for a small, local restaurant. These can be found all over the country and offer delicious food at an affordable price. English probably will not be spoken here, but I strongly recommend giving them a try. Dishes to try here are called Casados, which means "married." They usually come with your choice of a protein, alongside rice and beans, plantains, and a small salad. Pair that with a delicious batido (fruit smoothie) and you're in for a treat!

Another food you need to try at a Soda are Patacones, also known as Tostones in other parts of the Caribbean and Latin America, which are twice fried plantains. They are often served with ground black beans, guacamole or even ceviche for a tasty beach snack. 10/10 would recommend!

27. A hearty Costa Rican breakfast

Gallo Pinto is a seasoned rice and bean dish. The name translates to "Spotted Rooster" because of the appearance of the dark beans mixed with the white rice. It is typically served with eggs, local cheese, sour cream, a tortilla, and plantains. Don't forget the Costa Rican coffee!

28. WHAT TO DO IF YOU'RE GLUTEN INTOLERANT

While finding gluten free options in restaurants can't be guaranteed, here are some tips to help you navigate the gluten free options. Many traditional dishes like Casados are made with a seasoning called Consume. This is NOT gluten free. I recommend asking if their dishes have this ingredient, even if the menu says it is gluten free, to be on the safe side. With that said, many local restaurants won't label their menu with a gluten free symbol, but in more touristy restaurants, you're more likely to find gluten free foods. Gallo Pinto is a good breakfast option because the ingredients used don't contain gluten. Salsa Lizano, a popular sauce you'll find on the tables in restaurants, is also gluten free! I recommend

>TOURIST

downloading a gluten free card in Spanish ahead of time and saving it as an image on your phone in case you find yourself in a restaurant with no English speakers.

29. TIPS FOR VEGETARIANS/VEGANS

Fortunately for most vegetarians and vegans, the rice and beans are naturally vegetarian or vegan so this can be a go-to selection at most restaurants. You can also ask that the meat, eggs, and cheese that are included in Casado or Gallo Pinto be substituted with fruit, tortillas, vegetables, and more. A popular dish called Arroz con Vegetales is also a great lunch/dinner option that will be vegetarian or vegan friendly. Lastly, Costa Rica has an abundance of fruit and local supermarkets sell gluten free products! Check out the local fruit & veggie stands to buy fresh produce and prepare your meals at your accommodation.

WHAT SHOULD I DO IF I...?

30. NEED TO SEE A DOCTOR?

You can access private healthcare throughout the country, see a doctor in most pharmacies, and even buy important medications over the counter. Costa Rica is known for its quality and affordable healthcare so it's also a popular destination for medical tourism. Data from 2016 show that Costa Rica welcomed around 70,000 medical tourists. Primary procedures are dentistry and cosmetic surgery,[7] although you will find experts across many specialties here. My grandmother came here for a dental procedure, saving her almost 50% on dental implants, which is extremely costly in the United States.

In Guanacaste, there are several private clinics and 24-hour emergency care available. Rates for many medical services here are cheaper than the US even when paying out of pocket, so a trip to urgent care for

---

[7] https://howlermag.com/Costa-Rica-medical-tourism-industry

a couple stitches won't break the bank (phew!). However, travel health insurance is still a good idea to have in case you need an ambulance or something more serious happens. Major hospitals can be far away (1-2 hours) from many popular tourist destinations so keep that in mind. While we're on the subject, 911 is what you dial for emergencies.

31. SEE AN ANIMAL IN NEED?

Sadly, there are problems here with animal abuse and neglect, just like everywhere else. Many dogs and cats may be strays and roam the streets freely. The cat population is especially difficult to control so you will likely encounter some feral cats. However, most animals you see, especially if they look like they are a reasonably healthy weight and have a collar (even if they don't have a name tag) have an owner! So, no need to feel bad for them because these animals have a home and are allowed to roam freely. These dog and cats know all the best spots to get some love and attention from animal lovers visiting their town and of course, *eat your leftovers*.

If you see an animal that is clearly sick or injured, there are veterinary hospitals and animal rescues you can contact. Veterinary care is also very good, like human healthcare is! I also encourage you to learn about what local rescues may be doing in a particular community. For example, Barbara's Animal Rescue in Flamingo offers low cost spay and neuter clinics on a monthly basis. If you are looking for a way to contribute to animal welfare, you can donate to these groups or volunteer to walk the adoptable dogs.

A PERFECT BEACH DAY:

32. WHERE TO SURF

Tamarindo and Playa Grande are famous for surfing. While both beaches are next to each other, you can actually take a lesson in Tamarindo and cross an estuary to Playa Grande. Playa Grande is best for intermediate to advanced surfers as the waves are known for being bigger. It is also a national park that attracts leatherback turtles! This beach is much less developed than Tamarindo, so it's nice to see for surfers and beach goers alike. If you're lucky you may see some turtles laying their eggs or hatching too.

>TOURIST

Tamarindo is best for beginners and surfers looking to learn some turns and drop in on bigger waves. If you take a group surfing lesson here most tour guides guarantee, you'll stand up on the board during your first lesson. I like those odds!

Other popular beaches for surfing are Playa Avellanas, Marbella, Guiones, Witch's Rock, and Playa Santa Teresa.

33. WHAT TO BRING WITH YOU (AND LEAVE AT THE HOTEL)

You can rent chairs and tents that provide shade at many beaches, but usually the most frequented ones. If you're a little bit off the beaten path, pack a cooler with some food and drinks. You can also buy pipa fria (cold coconut), granizados (it's like a snow cone *or snowball, for the NOLA folks*) from vendors on the beach – the perfect beverage to keep you hydrated and refreshed all day long!

To safeguard your valuables, don't bring anything you'd be upset about losing. If you bring things like your wallets, phones, and Bluetooth speaker, always have someone staying with your stuff.

Bug spray is also handy to have because as the sun starts to go down, mosquitos and other pesky bugs become more active. There's nothing worse than trying to enjoy the sunset while getting attacked by mosquitoes or no-see-ums.

Lastly, make sure you have plenty of sunscreen!

One important note, many beaches don't have lifeguards or public restrooms. If you're visiting a beach for the day, plan your bathroom breaks strategically in case there isn't one nearby.

34. WATCH THE SUNSET

The sunsets draw everyone to the beach. You will see people congregating as soon as the sunset is about to begin, taking photos and *oohing* and *aahing* at the sky as the colors change. The sunsets typically begin between 5:00 and 6:00 PM year-round, so plan your beachside happy hours accordingly. There's a saying around here that if you blink, you'll miss the sunset because they don't last *that* long. The good news is they're predictable and there's no such thing as a bad sunset here.

>TOURIST

Some of the best restaurants to view the sunset are Coco Loco in Playa Flamingo, Sentido Norte (Call ahead and make a reservation for 5pm) in Las Catalinas, Volcano Brewing in Tamarindo, Patagonia Del Mar or Camaron Dorado in Brasilito, and Beach House or the Costa Rican Sailing Center in Potrero. However, there's no bad place to see the sunset either, so lay out your beach towel and take a seat on the beach wherever you are and take in the view.

TOP PLACES TO VISIT AND THINGS TO DO:

35. PLAYA CONCHAL

This is one of Costa Rica's most beloved beaches and it's only about an hour from the Liberia airport! The sand is made up of small crushed shells that shift around under your feet. The water is crystal blue, with small relaxing waves. It's obvious why this is one of the most popular beaches for locals and tourists alike. The whole beach is bordered by the

Reserva Conchal resort, so unless you're staying there you walk down the beach into Playa Conchal.

There are two options for parking. You can park in the town of Brasilito along the street. There are parking attendants there that will expect you to pay them for watching your car, although they are not an official security service. Your other option is to park at the parking lot that is right outside of Brasilito and take a shuttle. This parking is free, secure with cameras and a security guard, and there are bathrooms, showers, and changing rooms available there.

At Playa Conchal, you will find great snorkeling, howler monkeys swaying in the trees, and an opportunity to buy some souvenirs or snacks on the beach.

36. PLAYA BRASILITO

While visiting Playa Conchal, you might as well check out the town of Brasilito and the beach. It is a traditional Costa Rican town, formerly a fishing village, that attracts tourists from all over Costa Rica

>TOURIST

and internationally because of its proximity to Playa Conchal. During high season and Semana Santa, this little town gets inundated with traffic and beach goers. This is by far my favorite beach town! The people, the beaches, the sunsets, and the Sodas are all amazing in this town. If you're looking for the best place to try Casado and patacones, look no further than Soda Brasilito. It's in the plaza in front of Playa Brasilito next to the souvenir shops. Anytime I'm craving Costa Rican food, this is my go-to every time. Be sure to grab an iced coffee at Deli Cafe or check out the beach front, Patagonia del Mar restaurant for some sushi, live music, and the sunset. It's warm lighting and live music at night, make this restaurant irresistibly cozy and inviting.

37. PLAYA TAMARINDO

Tamarindo also began as a fishing village and has since developed into one of the most popular tourist destinations in Costa Rica. It has a wide variety of restaurants, beach activities for people of all ages, excursions, and accommodations. The main stretch that runs along the beach also has boutiques and art galleries. This beach is also known for its surfing, so a popular activity is to take a surf lesson.

What sets this town apart from nearby beach towns is the buzzing nightlife. Tamarindo has live entertainment most nights, night clubs, music festivals and dancing throughout the year. This town is a great place to stay if you're looking for somewhere that offers a variety of options while being centrally located for excursions throughout Guanacaste. If you're looking for a quieter town, I recommend neighboring towns of Playa Grande, Brasilito, Flamingo and Potrero or Coco.

38. PLAYA SAMARA

This little beach town has a more local feel, while offering plenty of amenities. This beach is the perfect family getaway or retreat, especially for those looking for something a little bit more laid back. It's further from LIR airport but still only a two-hour drive, making it convenient to get to. The drive itself is also beautiful with its picturesque rolling hills lined with palm trees.

Compared to the northern pacific beach towns of Tamarindo, Grande, Brasilito, Flamingo, and Potrero,

>TOURIST

Samara is unique for its centrally located downtown and the thick tropical dry forest surrounding it. It has calm water due to a reef that's close to shore, making it perfect for swimming and activities. There is also a great private reserve just outside Samara, the Werner-Sauter Biological Reserve, where you can take a tour of the tropical dry forest, see tons of wildlife and get some exercise. It is a moderate to difficult hike. Diving, snorkeling, surfing, and stand up paddle boarding are also popular activities in this town.

39. PLAYA NOSARA

Free your mind and find your center about an hour north of Samara in the town of Nosara. It is one of Costa Rica's most popular beach towns for yoga retreats. This village is located on the Nicoya peninsula which is one of the 5 blue zones in the world.[8] Blue zones are geographic areas with high concentrations of people that are 100 years old or older. If you're looking for an area where a healthy lifestyle, diet, and a positive relationship with nature is a priority for locals, then this is your spot! This

---

[8] https://www.nosara.com/secrets-nicoyan-long-life/

town also has access to some noteworthy beaches like Playa Guiones which is known for its long surf break, and Playa Pelada which has a reef offshore perfect for snorkeling and scuba diving.

40. SEA TURTLE "ARRIBADA" AT OSTIONAL WILDLIFE REFUGE

A trip to Costa Rica is not complete without sea turtles. Ostional is a small beach town and also a protected nesting site for thousands of Olive Ridley Sea Turtles each year. In fact, this is one of the most popular beaches to see sea turtles on the Pacific coast. You can stay in this town in order to ensure you see the turtles when they arrive to nest and enjoy some food at a nearby restaurant after your guided tour of the beach. Because it is a protected area, you can't go on the beach without a guide when sea turtles are nesting. This is to protect the nests as sea turtles are very sensitive to bright colors and light. It's quite a trek driving into Ostional, so this is a town where I highly recommend having a 4x4 vehicle. The roads are steep, rocky and unpaved, and likely to be muddy with some river crossings. Getting to Ostional is an adventure in itself, but the sea turtles are definitely a once in a lifetime opportunity.

41. MONTEVERDE CLOUD FOREST

Although many people are attracted to Costa Rica for its beautiful beaches, I am a firm believer that you can't come to Costa Rica without getting the full experience. This means the town of Monteverde *has* to be on your list. Monteverde is in Puntarenas province and easily accessible from San Jose or Liberia airports and just a three-hour drive from Tamarindo. Monteverde is more than just a beautiful mountain town, it is home to one of the rarest habitats on earth, the Cloud Forest. Here you will see an abundance of wildlife including night hikes where you will see sloths, snakes, butterflies, birds, and wildlife of all kinds. During the day, hike through misty, jungle-y trails of the Cloud Forests brimming with flora and fauna, birds, and insects. The trails are for the most part an easy walk, however the pathways can be slick and muddy, so I suggest having water resistant hiking boots and a lightweight rain jacket.

This community is also a major ecotourism destination, for its coffee and chocolate farms, and sustainable farming in the region. This is another place I recommend having a 4x4 vehicle because of the steep grades as you drive up in elevation to get to Monteverde. The roads getting up there are also not paved, very rocky, and muddy because of the rainfall.

42. DIRIA COFFEE FARM TOUR

Coffee lovers rejoice because there is a great coffee farm tour just an hour and a half away from LIR airport. This tour is a fun experience where you will learn about Costa Rica's coffee farming industry, the process of growing coffee, and what makes Costa Rica's coffee so special. Top it all off with samples of Costa Rican coffee and purchase a bag or three to take home with you! The coffee is all produced in Guanacaste, comprised of a cooperative organization of small producers.

>TOURIST

BEST HIKING SPOTS, WATERFALLS & HOT SPRINGS:

43. LLANOS DE CORTEZ WATERFALL

Guanacaste doesn't have as many waterfalls as other regions of the country, so it can be hard to check seeing waterfalls off your bucket list. However, this waterfall is only 30 minutes from Liberia airport, great for kids, and easily accessible. The trail down to the base of the waterfall is made up of steps with a handrail, making it an easy walk down. I recommend packing a picnic for a day of splashing around in the swimming hole, cliff jumping off a nearby (and smaller) waterfall and cooling off in the Guanacaste heat.

44. LAS CATALINAS

This beach town is a new development site, north of Tamarindo with a network of hiking and mountain biking trails. As you navigate the trails, you will see panoramic views of the ocean as well as have the opportunity to take a dip in the ocean at a nearby beach. Driving into Las Catalinas, there is a parking lot at the very end, which brings you to the starting point of the hiking trails. You can spend as little or as much time as you want on these trails, but one thing is for sure, you will build up a sweat! Bring a water bottle and wear your swimsuit under your workout clothes so you can cool off with a swim in the ocean afterward. I also recommend having your phone with you so you can take pictures of the beautiful views of the ocean as you weave along the coastline. In the town itself, there is a restaurant, public bathrooms, and some beach activities so you can make an entire day of it.

45. RINCON DE LA VIEJA

This national park is a must visit when in Guanacaste, especially if you want to hike 2 volcanoes, go river rafting, camping, and soak in the natural hot springs. For hiking enthusiasts, the dry season is the best time to visit as the conditions of the trails will be the best at this time. Along these trails you can see a wide variety of flora and fauna as well as boiling mud pots, waterfalls and lagoons. One of the hikes, goes directly up Rincon de la Vieja

Volcano and will take about a da_
in mind this is an active volcano s(
some restrictions and requires adequ
After your hike, relax your muscles i)
springs and rejuvenate your skin with ₍   ₎ud
mask. Don't forget to stay hydrated though!

46. ARENAL VOLCANO & TOWN OF LA FORTUNA

Arenal is another prominent active volcano with hiking trails, lava fields and hot springs. The town of La Fortuna is close to this volcano which is another popular mountain town for tourists and hiking/nature enthusiasts. Within this quaint town, there are many restaurants, accommodations, and La Fortuna Waterfall. La Fortuna waterfall is a popular waterfall in Costa Rica – but if you're into photography, make sure you get there early to beat the crowds for the perfect photo.

CHOOSE YOUR ADVENTURE:

47. ADVENTURE TRAVEL

Costa Rica is such a popular country for tourism because it has something that appeals to everyone, especially adventure! From ziplining to white water rafting, to sport fishing and scuba diving, there is no shortage of activities for thrill seekers. Diamante Eco Adventure park offers the longest zipline in Costa Rica at a mile long! There, you can also visit an animal sanctuary, butterfly observatory, and botanical garden. At most beach towns, you will be able to find kayak and stand up paddle boarding, ATV tours, horseback riding, and jet ski rentals.

48. VOLUNTEERING IN COSTA RICA

Whether its conservation and working with animals like sea turtles, jaguars, or sloths, teaching English or working with kids, or providing medical care, there are many opportunities to volunteer in Costa Rica. Just make sure you do your research to identify opportunities that are responsible, ethical, transparent, and respectful of local culture. Amigos of Costa Rica, Corcovado Foundation, and Costa Rica Wildlife Sanctuary are a few options worth looking into. If you're interested in getting involved in the Brasilito and Potrero communities, Abriendo Mentes is an education and community development non-profit dedicated to improving education opportunities for youth, including providing computer classes and English classes which are crucial skills for their future. WWOOFing may also be another option if you're interested in working on a farm in exchange for free accommodation.

49. NAMASTE OR *NAW, IMMA STAY* (IN COSTA RICA)?

Costa Rica is a top destination for yoga retreats and wellness centers which makes sense given its 'pura vida' reputation, amiright? They are especially popular along the coast of Guanacaste. Hotspots for yoga retreats in Guanacaste include Tamarindo, Playa Negra, and Nosara. There is no doubt that Costa Rica is a top destination for a yoga retreat, given its beautiful natural surroundings, tropical fruit and vegan/vegetarian friendly food options and natural and healthy lifestyle.

50. LGBTQ+ TRAVEL

Costa Rica is considered to be tolerant of LGBTQ+, although it is still predominately conservative, Roman Catholic. If you're looking for specifically LGBTQ+ friendly hotels, for example, they are mostly concentrated in San Jose and some in Manuel Antonio. While both of these places are located outside of Guanacaste province, they are about a four-hour drive from Tamarindo, making them easily accessible from the region. Manuel Antonio is considered a hotspot for gay men in Costa Rica, however, the International LGBTQ+ Travel Association (IGLTA) says it caters more to gay men than women, trans or non-binary people. When planning your trip to Costa Rica, I recommend IGLTA's website as a starting point to learn more about Costa Rica's attitudes and political landscape surrounding LGBTQ+.

\>TOURIST

TOP REASONS TO BOOK THIS TRIP

1. The variety of nature and wildlife is unmatched

2. Pristine beaches & beautiful coastline

3. The culture & *Pura Vida* lifestyle

>TOURIST

BONUS TIPS

Couldn't get enough of Costa Rica? Here's a beginner's guide to everything you need to know about living the *pura vida* life:

CAN I LEGALLY WORK IN COSTA RICA?

The short answer is no. Costa Rica does offer a work visa, but they are intentionally hard to get. You must have a skill that no other Costa Rican has to justify the visa. The only other option is to become a permanent resident. This is possible if you buy property and invest a certain amount, you are then eligible to apply for residency. However, as a resident, you are only allowed to own a business, but you are not allowed to work at it and instead, you must hire Ticos to do the work. There are a couple different options so consult a lawyer to discuss which option is right for you.

HOW DOES A TOURIST VISA WORK?

On a tourist visa, US passport holders are granted 90 days in Costa Rica. Many people living in Costa Rica stay on a tourist visa and simply renew their visa every 90 days before it expires. This option is usually recommended to people coming to Costa Rica to try it out or for people to visit several times in different places before deciding on a place to live. However, these rules can change at any time.

CAN I BUY A CAR IN COSTA RICA?

You can buy a car here! The process can be a little bit tricky, especially if you don't speak Spanish. The most important thing to know before buying a car is that they are heavily taxed and thus very expensive. Prices for cars will be up to 2 times as much as their price in the United States. If you are thinking of importing a car, there are some plus sides to doing this but usually saving money is not one of them, as they are heavily taxed upon importation into Costa Rica.

>TOURIST

CAN I BRING MY PETS WITH ME?

Costa Rica is very pet friendly and flying into the country with them is an achievable feat. I won't say it's easy, because much of it depends on the animal you're bringing and the breed. For cats and small dogs, there a few less hoops to jump through because they can fly with you on the plane. For larger dogs, who may need to go in the cargo, you will likely need a pet shipper which makes this endeavor much more expensive. However, I moved here with a large dog, hired a pet shipper and also brought a cat with me. If I can do it, anyone can!

WHERE DO EXPATS LIVE?

There are many expat enclaves all over Costa Rica including Tamarindo, Flamingo, Potrero, and Coco! Whether you're looking to join them, or avoid them, I recommend joining Costa Rica Facebook groups for expats to begin your research and talk to expats living in Costa Rica.

>TOURIST

PACKING AND PLANNING TIPS

A Week before Leaving

- Arrange for someone to take care of pets and water plants.
- Email and Print important Documents.
- Get Visa and vaccines if needed.
- Check for travel warnings.
- Stop mail and newspaper.
- Notify Credit Card companies where you are going.
- Passports and photo identification is up to date.
- Pay bills.
- Copy important items and download travel Apps.
- Start collecting small bills for tips.
- Have post office hold mail while you are away.
- Check weather for the week.
- Car inspected, oil is changed, and tires have the correct pressure.
- Check airline luggage restrictions.
- Download Apps needed for your trip.

Right Before Leaving

- Contact bank and credit cards to tell them your location.
- Clean out refrigerator.
- Empty garbage cans.
- Lock windows.
- Make sure you have the proper identification with you.
- Bring cash for tips.
- Remember travel documents.
- Lock door behind you.
- Remember wallet.
- Unplug items in house and pack chargers.
- Change your thermostat settings.
- Charge electronics, and prepare camera memory cards.

>TOURIST

READ OTHER GREATER THAN A TOURIST BOOKS

Greater Than a Tourist- Geneva Switzerland: 50 Travel Tips from a Local by Amalia Kartika

Greater Than a Tourist- St. Croix US Birgin Islands USA: 50 Travel Tips from a Local by Tracy Birdsall

Greater Than a Tourist- San Juan Puerto Rico: 50 Travel Tips from a Local by Melissa Tait

Greater Than a Tourist – Lake George Area New York USA: 50 Travel Tips from a Local by Janine Hirschklau

Greater Than a Tourist – Monterey California United States: 50 Travel Tips from a Local by Katie Begley

Greater Than a Tourist – Chanai Crete Greece: 50 Travel Tips from a Local by Dimitra Papagrigoraki

Greater Than a Tourist – The Garden Route Western Cape Province South Africa: 50 Travel Tips from a Local by Li-Anne McGregor van Aardt

Greater Than a Tourist – Sevilla Andalusia Spain: 50 Travel Tips from a Local by Gabi Gazon

Children's Book: *Charlie the Cavalier Travels the World* by Lisa Rusczyk Ed. D.

> TOURIST

Follow us on Instagram for beautiful travel images:
http://Instagram.com/GreaterThanATourist

Follow *Greater Than a Tourist* on Amazon.
>Tourist Podcast
>T Website
>T Youtube
>T Facebook
>T Goodreads
>T Amazon
>T Mailing List
>T Pinterest
>T Instagram
>T Twitter
>T SoundCloud
>T LinkedIn
>T Map

> TOURIST

At *Greater Than a Tourist*, we love to share travel tips with you. How did we do? What guidance do you have for how we can give you better advice for your next trip? Please send your feedback to GreaterThanaTourist@gmail.com as we continue to improve the series. We appreciate your constructive feedback. Thank you.

>TOURIST

METRIC CONVERSIONS

TEMPERATURE

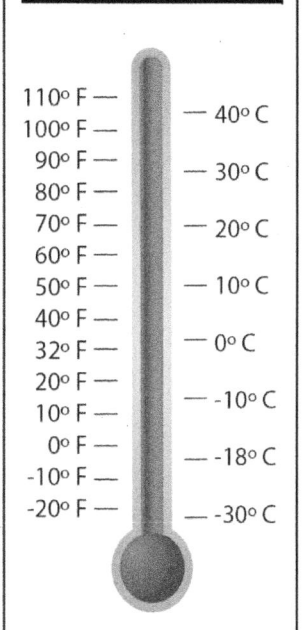

110° F — — 40° C
100° F —
90° F — — 30° C
80° F —
70° F — — 20° C
60° F —
50° F — — 10° C
40° F —
32° F — — 0° C
20° F —
10° F — — -10° C
0° F —
-10° F — — -18° C
-20° F — — -30° C

To convert F to C:

Subtract 32, and then multiply by 5/9 or .5555.

To Convert C to F:

Multiply by 1.8 and then add 32.

32F = 0C

LIQUID VOLUME

To Convert:................Multiply by
U.S. Gallons to Liters................ 3.8
U.S. Liters to Gallons 26
Imperial Gallons to U.S. Gallons 1.2
Imperial Gallons to Liters....... 4.55
Liters to Imperial Gallons 22
1 Liter = .26 U.S. Gallon
1 U.S. Gallon = 3.8 Liters

DISTANCE

To convert ....Multiply by
Inches to Centimeters 2.54
Centimeters to Inches 39
Feet to Meters...................... .3
Meters to Feet 3.28
Yards to Meters 91
Meters to Yards 1.09
Miles to Kilometers 1.61
Kilometers to Miles............ .62
1 Mile = 1.6 km
1 km = .62 Miles

WEIGHT

1 Ounce = .28 Grams
1 Pound = .4555 Kilograms
1 Gram = .04 Ounce
1 Kilogram = 2.2 Pounds

81

>TOURIST

TRAVEL QUESTIONS

- Do you bring presents home to family or friends after a vacation?
- Do you get motion sick?
- Do you have a favorite billboard?
- Do you know what to do if there is a flat tire?
- Do you like a sun roof open?
- Do you like to eat in the car?
- Do you like to wear sun glasses in the car?
- Do you like toppings on your ice cream?
- Do you use public bathrooms?
- Did you bring a cell phone and does it have power?
- Do you have a form of identification with you?
- Have you ever been pulled over by a cop?
- Have you ever given money to a stranger on a road trip?
- Have you ever taken a road trip with animals?
- Have you ever gone on a vacation alone?
- Have you ever run out of gas?

- If you could move to any place in the world, where would it be?
- If you could travel anywhere in the world, where would you travel?
- If you could travel in any vehicle, which one would it be?
- If you had three things to wish for from a magic genie, what would they be?
- If you have a driver's license, how many times did it take you to pass the test?
- What are you the most afraid of on vacation?
- What do you want to get away from the most when you are on vacation?
- What foods smell bad to you?
- What item do you bring on ever trip with you away from home?
- What makes you sleepy?
- What song would you love to hear on the radio when you're cruising on the highway?
- What travel job would you want the least?
- What will you miss most while you are away from home?
- What is something you always wanted to try?

>TOURIST

- What is the best road side attraction that you ever saw?
- What is the farthest distance you ever biked?
- What is the farthest distance you ever walked?
- What is the weirdest thing you needed to buy while on vacation?
- What is your favorite candy?
- What is your favorite color car?
- What is your favorite family vacation?
- What is your favorite food?
- What is your favorite gas station drink or food?
- What is your favorite license plate design?
- What is your favorite restaurant?
- What is your favorite smell?
- What is your favorite song?
- What is your favorite sound that nature makes?
- What is your favorite thing to bring home from a vacation?
- What is your favorite vacation with friends?
- What is your favorite way to relax?
- Where is the farthest place you ever traveled in a car?

- Where is the farthest place you ever went North, South, East and West?
- Where is your favorite place in the world?
- Who is your favorite singer?
- Who taught you how to drive?
- Who will you miss the most while you are away?
- Who if the first person you will contact when you get to your destination?
- Who brought you on your first vacation?
- Who likes to travel the most in your life?
- Would you rather be hot or cold?
- Would you rather drive above, below, or at the speed limited?
- Would you rather drive on a highway or a back road?
- Would you rather go on a train or a boat?
- Would you rather go to the beach or the woods?

>TOURIST

TRAVEL BUCKET LIST

1.

2.

3.

4.

5.

6.

7.

8.

9.

10.

\>TOURIST

NOTES

Printed in Great Britain
by Amazon